HAGGADAH

A MESSIANIC SEDER

Remembering The Testimony
From Slavery To Freedom
God's Redemptive Story

METRO JEWISH RESOURCES

©2019 Rabbi Felix Halpern
Metro Jewish Resources
All Rights Reserved
No reproduction without the permission
from Metro Jewish Resources

Rabbi Felix Halpern, Founder of Metro Jewish Resources
Haggadah 2019 Project Creator and Director
Contributing Editor

Rabbi Sharon David Shubin-Moss
Haggadah 2019 Project Designer
Contributing Editor

www.metrojewishag.org

The MJR Messianic Haggadah guides its reader in a step by step celebration of the Passover Seder through a clear easy to follow experience. It has been Metro Jewish Resources highest mitzvah to serve others in this endeavor.

This Haggadah was created to serve you as an invaluable inspirational resource. It fulfills our observation in Jewish tradition of one of the most important Festival's in the Torah, and brings to light the ancient historical testimony of the Hebrew people.

The Passover and its importance transcend time. Through this Haggadah and the Passover Seder, God's story of redemption for His people emerges in a dramatic step by step foretelling of a timeless story, while engaging every participant, both young and old.

While fostering a biblical foundation through the understanding of the historical, cultural and religious framework of Israel and the Jewish people, this Haggadah serves Jewish and Gentile communities in their common foundation. MJR operates in the spirit of Tikkun Olam. We trust that you discover the richness of this Haggadah and its treasure of Biblical truths and Torah principles.

תודה רבה
TODA RABA
Thank You So Very Much

Metro Jewish Resources gratefully recognizes the contributions of our entire Metro Family Team for their gracious outpouring of gifts, skills, prayer and hospitality.

Thank you so very much for your sacrifice of giving in the true spirit of Mitzvot toward this first Messianic Haggadah Project of the MJR ministry.
Baruch Hashem.

B'H ~ This mark indicates that references to the name of God are included within this document. We ask that you care and respect this document out of reverence for the name of The LORD.

Order of The Seder

The Passover	8
Chametz	12
Preparing The Seder	14
Shehecheyanu	15
Elements & Symbols	16
Yom Tov Candles	18
The Four Cups	19
Cup Of Sanctification	20
Cup Of Elijah	23
Urchatz	23
Karpas	25
Mah Nishtanah	27
The Matzah	30
Yachatz	32
Maror	36
Korech & Charoset	38
Why Do We Recline?	39
Maggid	40
Cup Of Plagues	44
Passover Lamb	49
Zeroah	50
Beitzah, The Khagigah	51
Dayenu	53
Shulkhan Oreykh	55
Afikoman	56
Cup Of Redemption	57
Cup Of Elijah	59
Cup Of Praise	61
Nirtzah	63

B'H

THE HAGGADAH

A MESSIANIC SEDER

פֶּסַח
THE PASSOVER

'This day shall be a memorial for you, keep it as a feast to The LORD throughout your generations, you will keep this feast forever. Seven days you will eat unleavened bread, and you will remove all leaven from your home, and whoever eats leavened bread, that soul will be cut off from Israel.'
EXODUS 12:14-15

LEADER

Judaism is a religion and culture based on memory. From one festival to another, Jews are reminded of what brought them to the land of Israel so many years ago, and how they have survived throughout their history.

Passover is a day devoted to remembrance, as well as to obedience. It is God's command to honor the Passover forever!

Passover is the first of the three great annual festivals. At God's direction, Passover is held in the spring, from the 14th to the 21st days in the month of Nisan. This Hebrew month begins the Spiritual New Year.

'It shall be the first month of the year to you.'
The command is given to keep the Passover in Jerusalem, the location God chose to place His name.

There are several distinct passages relating to the Passover in Exodus and Deuteronomy, where the original concepts of unleavened bread, the paschal lamb, and the firstborn sanctified are mentioned. There is great prophetic significance to each of these elements.
The Passover was a time designed by The Father for Yeshua to fulfill. In it we see the course of events that

would unfold during the last days of his ministry. As he stepped through each prescribed element of the feast, his full identity became prophetically evident.

Written in Exodus 23:15 we see The Feast of Unleavened Bread. In Exodus 23:18 and 34:25 we see God refer to the Paschal Lamb as My Sacrifice. In Exodus 4:22-23 God calls Israel, My Firstborn Son. And in Exodus 13:11-16 the teaching of the Redemption of the Firstborn is remembered.

In Exodus 5:1 God begins His Plan for Redemption.

> *'Moses and Aaron went and told Pharaoh, The Lord God of Israel said, Let my people go, that they may hold a feast unto me in the wilderness.'*

The great 'I AM' who had commissioned Moses with this task at the burning bush, was setting in motion an unimaginable sequence of miracles, to be remembered and celebrated perpetually. Only God knew, how many centuries later, this feast would culminate in the sacrifice of 'The Lamb of God', the Messiah of Israel, Yeshua.

Preparation for the first Passover, while the Israelite slaves were still in Egypt, required that each Hebrew household roast a lamb. The lamb was required to be roasted whole and great care was taken that not one bone of the sacrificial lamb should be broken.

The blood of the sacrifice was to be sprinkled on their doorposts, so that the life of the firstborn from each family would be spared. The entire lamb was to be eaten that same night, along with bitter herbs. Any remaining portion of the feast was to be burned.

The Israelites ate unleavened bread with the lamb because there was no time for their bread to rise. They would be leaving their life of bondage abruptly and in haste. As a remembrance today, the unleavened bread is a tangible symbol of the reality that The Great 'I AM' delivered His people quickly and mightily.

This reality has been commemorated for thousands of years until this vary day. Preceding the onset of the yearly Passover the removal of yeast is undertaken, connoting a fresh start at the beginning of the spiritual year. This takes place just prior to the first offering of the barley harvest unto The Lord, ensuring a yeast-free offering. Until this day, only unleavened bread is eaten throughout the entire festival week.

The ceremonial Passover meal came to be known as the Seder meal. Seder is a Hebrew word which means Order. The whole evening revolves around the steps of telling of the story of the Exodus of the Israelite people out of Egypt. The entire ceremony unfolds like acts in a play. Filled with drama, the Seder Plate invites participation and learning for all ages.

Passover has been referred to as the Crown Jewel of the Lord's feasts. The remembrance of this momentous historical event is the highlight of the Spiritual New Year.

Passover is also known as the feast of unity, because through the Messiah our Deliverer, God has conquered our enemies in the same manner as he led Moses through the wilderness, parted the Red Sea, and fed our people with Manna from heaven.

Upon these foundational truths we prepare our hearts to engage our history, as we engage one another.

Did you know?...
- The Hebrew name for Passover is PESACH, which roughly means 'he had pity, skip, omit, or pass over'. It is thought that God had pity on the Israelites in Egypt and passed over their houses, because they obeyed his warning to them.

ζ Two thousand years ago it was recorded, that when the people looked at the fields surrounding Jerusalem, there was such a multitude of lambs gathered, ready for the Passover, the city appeared to be wrapped in a blanket of pure white fleece.

ζ Matzah must remain in motion to keep it from fermenting. Bakers have 18 minutes from the time they add water till they put the Matzah in the ovens before it becomes Chametz, leavened. There are only an estimated 20 Matzah factories who bake Passover Matzah for the entire world.

ζ As we step through the Seder we can reflect on our own journey to this place. Like the Israelites, we all have spent our lives, busy building something for someone. But what is the value of what we have built? That depends on the materials we have used, and what it has cost us. Was it worth it, was it all sweet, or was it all bitter? Our life with God is both, it is bittersweet.

ζ The Passover is a time to look dimly into the ancient past, hoping to see ourselves more clearly in the Light of God's Story. At best, our story has been like the Seder Plate's Korech, an unusual sandwich of bitter herbs like Maror, held together with Kharoset, the spiced mortar of sweet fruits of The Lords presence before us and behind us within our every step.

חמץ

CHAMETZ

Hebrew Word For Leaven

You shall eat nothing chametz,
in all your habitations you will eat matzah.
EXODUS 12:20

LEADER

Passover asks us to do one simple thing, Tell the Story. Tell the story of how God's people, enslaved and oppressed, were brought out from bondage and made into a great nation.

For this to occur much preparation is involved. Part of the traditional preparation for Passover in every Jewish home is the search and removal of yeast, or Chametz. Every corner of the house is swept and cleaned. This is mostly observed in orthodox and observant Jewish homes. It is important that during Passover we refrain from eating Chametz, as no leaven is allowed in the home.

This tradition reminds us of the fact that the Hebrews had no time to let their bread rise as they made their hurried escape from Egypt.

> *For seven days you will eat unleavened bread; and from the first day you will remove all leaven out of your houses, and whoever eats leavened bread from the first to the seventh day, that soul shall be cut off from Israel. Exodus 12:15*

With the home prepared and the table set, everyone gathers around the Passover table. It begins with the reading of The Haggadah, which means The Telling. Afterward, a traditional and familiar invitation is given.

> *'Let all who are poor come and eat,*
> *let all who are in need come and make the Passover.'*

The words of this Traditional Passover Blessing have been recited by Jewish people for thousands of years. Yeshua, offered a similar invitation.

> *'Come to Me, all who are weary and heavy laden,*
> *and I will give you rest.'* Matthew 11:28

Always remember, the most important goal of the Passover is to tell the story of God's miraculous deliverance. As we share The Haggadah, we recount our own transitions from slavery to freedom, despair to hope, from darkness to light.

We may not be slaves as the ancient Israelites in Egypt were, but when we come to faith in Messiah we too are truly liberated. We are freed from self and the sin and bondage of our humanity. We are given a life of freedom in this world, and the privilege of entering the redemptive world to come.

Did you know?...

- ζ As God cared for the children of Israel in ancient times, he cares for all who are His today. There are no children's tables at The Seder. There is a place and a purpose for each generation to gather as one around the Table.

- ζ These words, shall be in your heart. You will teach them to your children diligently; you will talk of them when you sit in your house, when you walk by the way, when you lie down, and when you rise up. And you shall love The LORD your God with all your heart, with all your soul, and with all your might.
Deuteronomy 6:5-7

PREPARING THE SEDER
Setting The Lord's Table

LEADER
The Seder Plate contains the ceremonial items which help us tell the story of the Exodus. Taking part in The Seder makes the Passover a memorable experience.

The order of the service is set forth in The Haggadah. This service leads both the teller and the listener through the footsteps of the Israelites as we remember our own deliverance.

The Passover Seder is a sacred and inclusive night for all ages, from young to old.

The Seder Plate presents us with new and curious foods that are used to illustrate and connect us to the story. As we experience the taste of these symbolic foods, we take our own steps forward, seeing our own version of The Last Supper of the Israelites in Egypt.

Not unlike The Last Supper of Messiah Yeshua, we will taste God's goodness and remember the sweetness of his promises, and the bitterness of sin and separation.

This is The Lord's table beautifully set before us.

So, let us begin with the Shehecheyanu Blessing, the kindling of Yom Tov candles, the cups, the questions, the breaking of unleavened Matzah and the Seder Plate.

SHEHECHEYANU
Who Has Given Us Life

The Shehecheyanu Blessing is a Hebrew Prayer
recited over new and unusual experiences.
It is said at the beginning of special holidays and celebrations.
The Shehecheyanu Blessing is for thanking God for
allowing us to reach this day.

ALL RESPOND

Blessed are You, Adonai our God, Sovereign of all, who has kept us alive, sustained us, and brought us to this season.

Baruch Atah, Adonai Elo-heinu, Melech Ha-olam, she-heche-yanu v'kiy'manu v'higi-yanu laz'man hazeh.

ברוך אתה ה' א-לוהינו, מלך העולם, שהחינו וקימנו והגענו לזמן הזה.

Elements & Symbols
What Is That On The Seder Plate?

Seder Plate – Any plate large enough to present the six elements for the service, all on one plate to tell the story. Upon the Seder Plate will be the Maror, Karpas, Beitzah, Zeroah, Charoset, and Bitter Tears.

For a large group, more than one Seder Plate may be used. Or, groupings of the six elements may be set about for guests sitting beyond the head of the table to reach and partake of.

Maror – A small portion of bitter herbs, such as horseradish or raw onion, is set on the Seder Plate.

Karpas – A handful of spring greens, such as parsley, basil, or other leafy vegetable, is set on the Seder Plate.

Beitzah – A roasted hard-boiled egg is placed on the Seder Plate. This egg is also The Khagigah offering.

Zeroah – The shank bone of a roasted lamb is placed on the Seder Plate.

Kharoset – A sweet relish made of apples, nuts, spices and sweet kosher wine is placed on the Seder Plate.

Bitter Tears – A pint size bowl of salted water or mild vinegar is set near or centered on the Seder Plate.

Matzah Plate – A plate for the three Matzah breads is used during the Seder. The Matzah is covered with a white cloth or a Matzah Tash, a special cloth bag with three inner pockets, used during the Seder service.

Matzah – Unleavened bread, large cracker type breads baked without leaven. The bread is flat and striped with rows of piercings. Three Matzah breads are the minimum needed to conduct the service.

Elijah's Cup – A beautiful and unique cup, filled with the fruit of the vine, is set apart for this special prophetic guest.

The Four Cups – Prepare a single cup at each guests' place setting to be refilled four times; or four separate cups for each guest to be filled for each step in the Seder.

Fruit of the Vine – A decanter or pitcher of simple grape juice or a kosher wine is used. Enough to fill Elijah's Cup once, and the Four Cups to be filled the four times for each guest.

YOM TOV CANDLES
Lighting Of The Holiday Candles

The Lord is my light and my salvation,
Whom shall I fear?
PSALM 27:1

LEADER
Before the start of every Sabbath or Jewish holiday, it is traditional for the woman of the house, or another individual, to light two candles in honor of the holiness of the day.

Torah scholars teach it is the woman who is considered to be the one who reignites God's light in the home.

It is through her nurturing presence the woman guides her home into a place of holiness and peace. This is why it is her honor to kindle the Yom Tov lights, creating a separated and sacred space for her family and guests.

As the lights of the festival of redemption are kindled by the hand of a woman; let us remember that our promised Redeemer, the Light of the world, came into this world through the seed of a woman.

The lights are lit with a prayer for the illumination of the soul to come through God's Spirit. Remembering in Him is life, and His life was and is the Light of the world.

ALL RESPOND
We kindle the festival lights as we pray for illumination from the Spirit of God to bring us into a deeper personal understanding and meaning to this Passover celebration.

THE BLESSING OVER THE LIGHTS

» As a Woman, or another individual, Kindles the Yom Tov Lights, she alone recites this Blessing.

Blessed are You, Lord our God, King of the Universe, Who has sanctified us with His commandments and commanded us to kindle the Yom Tov Lights.

Baruch Atah, Adonai Elo-heinu, Melech Ha-olam,
asher kid' shanu b'mitzvotav v'tzivanu
l'hadlik ner *shel yom tov
        (or, *Shabbat v'shel)

בָּרוּךְ אַתָּה יְיָ אֱלֹהֵינוּ מֶלֶךְ הָעוֹלָם, אֲשֶׁר קִדְּשָׁנוּ בְּמִצְוֹתָיו,
וְצִוָּנוּ לְהַדְלִיק נֵר שֶׁל (שַׁבָּת וְשֶׁל) יוֹם טוֹב.

Did you know?...
ζ In Him was life, and his life was the light of the world. His light shines in the darkness, and the darkness has not overpowered it.

THE FOUR CUPS
Sanctification . Wrath . Redemption . Praise

Then the Lord said to Moses, 'Now you will see what I will do'
EXODUS 6:1

LEADER
As the Lord spoke an encouragement to Moses, The Lord revealed his plan by which he would redeem the people. Let us read the words that The Lord said to Moses.

ALL RESPOND
I will bring you out from under
    the yoke of the Egyptians,
I will free you from being slaves,
I will redeem you with an outstretched arm,
I will take you as my own people, and
I will be your God.
    Exodus 6:6-7

LEADER
At Passover, we celebrate God's promises of redemption and relationship by drinking from our cups four times. Each time representing one of The Four Cups of the Passover. With each cup, we recall the union that God desires, and has also preserved with the Jewish people.

Sanctification . Wrath . Redemption . Praise

קַדֵּשׁ
KADESH
CUP OF SANCTIFACTION

LEADER
Let us lift the Cup of Sanctification, the first cup of the Passover. Before we drink, let us all bless the name of The Lord for His provision, then we will drink.

ALL RESPOND
Blessed are You, O God, Ruler of the Universe, who creates the fruit of the vine.

Baruch Atah, Adonai Elo-heinu, Melech Ha-olam, borey p'ri hagafen.

בָּרוּךְ אַתָּה ה׳, אֱ-לֹהֵינוּ מֶלֶךְ הָעוֹלָם, בּוֹרֵא פְּרִי הַגֶּפֶן.

LEADER
God brought Israel out of captivity to set apart and sanctified a people unto himself. It is from these, God's people, the promised Messiah, our Savior, would come.

As Yeshua Messiah began his final Passover Seder he lifted and shared the cup with his disciples and said, 'Take this cup, divide it among you. I tell you I will not drink this cup again until the kingdom of God comes.'

Let us lift our first cup and drink together, as we join with the disciples, in celebrating God's faithful promises.

CUP OF ELIJAH

For The Prophet Eliyahu Ha Navi

Watch, I will send to you the Prophet Elijah
Before the coming dreadful Day of The LORD.
MALACHI 4:5

LEADER

We see The Fifth Cup, filled and ready, set apart for a special awaited guest. This is the Cup of Elijah. It is reserved for the final act of the Passover Seder.

It is Elijah who will come to announce the Day of The Messiah's arrival. He will come, sent from God, and announce the entrance of the Messiah the Son of David.

וּרְחַץ

URCHATZ
Ritual Hand Washing

'Who may ascend the hill of The LORD?
Who may stand in his holy place?
He who has clean hands and a pure heart.'
PSALM 24:3-4

LEADER

As the water washes over our hands, it is time to focus on our individual lives. Let us call to mind the importance of water to all life, both natural and spiritual.

'Do you understand what I have done for you?' He asked them. 'You call me Teacher and Lord, and rightfully so, for that is what I am. Now that I your Lord and Teacher, have washed your feet, you also should wash one another's feet.'

Let us share in the handwashing ceremony, or Urchatz. As we share the basin of water, let's reflect upon this gesture of humility and the lesson of commitment made by Yeshua.

It was on that night he laid aside his garments and girded himself with a towel. Then stooping, he poured water into a basin and began to wash his disciples' feet. Drying them with his towel, the Messiah said to them...

'If I, who is your Lord and Teacher, have washed your feet, then you also ought to wash one another's feet. For I have given you this example, that you should do as I have done for you.

Most assuredly, I say to you, a servant is not greater

than his master; nor is he who is sent greater than the one who sent him. If you know these things, then you will be blessed if you do them.'

Did you know?

- For the Urchatz, traditionally the water is poured over your right hand first. Then repeated for your left hand. This is the practice of the Kohanim, the High Priest's, as they prepared for entering the Temple to serve The Lord.

- In ancient biblical times it was customary that a host would provide water for guests to wash their feet, or provide a servant to wash the feet of their guests.

- In 1 Samuel 25:41 the scripture points to the first biblical passage where an honored person offers to wash the feet of another as a sign of humility. It is considered, the historical foot washing event that took place in John 13, began as a Jewish practice to honor their guests.

כַּרְפַּס
KARPAS
Tender Greens Of Spring

The Israelites groaned in their slavery and cried out for help, God heard their cries and remembered His promises to them.
EXODUS 2:23-24

LEADER

One reason given for dipping a vegetable into salt water is to provoke children to ask about it, this is a night for curiosities and questions. The story is to be recounted by way of questions and answers. Dipping a vegetable before a main meal is something different, thus it tickles and provokes the curios nature of the children.

Passover is a holiday that comes in the spring, when the earth is emerging from winter, green with new life. The Karpas is a symbol of all life created and sustained by Almighty God.

But life in Egypt for the Hebrews was full of suffering, and tears. The salt water is symbolic of a life immersed in tears.

Parsley, or celery, is dipped in salt water and then eaten. The Karpas symbolizes both the humble origins of the Hebrew people, and their renewal and rebirth like the greening of spring. Before dipping and eating the Karpas we recite the following blessing as we lift it up to God.

ALL RESPOND
Blessed are You, Lord our God, King of the Universe, who creates the fruit of the earth.

Baruch Atah, Adonai Elo-heinu, Melech Ha-olam, boreh pree ha'adamah.

בָּרוּךְ אַתָּה ה' אֱ-לֹהֵינוּ מֶלֶךְ הָעוֹלָם בּוֹרֵא פְּרִי הָאֲדָמָה.

MAH NISHTANAH
The Four Questions

'When your children ask you,
What does this ceremony mean to you?
Then tell them…'
EXODUS 12:26

LEADER

One of the highlights of the Passover is the participation of the children. Whether we are at home with family or gathering in a service with our community, including the children is welcome. And it is Mah Nishtanah, the four questions, that gives them a chance to ask, ask, ask, ask.

It is both a sacred act and a privilege to answer the four questions of Passover. It is our joy to tell the children of the mighty works of The God who keeps His Promises.

The Mah Nishtanah asks. Why is tonight different from all other nights? What unique power does this night hold to inspire the soul from generation to generation. God calls us all to his table tonight, from the hardened skeptic to the surrendered soul, he feeds us all. Tonight, we come forward, we lean back as we lean in, tonight we are hungry, thirsty, and curious, tonight we ask Why!

ALL RESPOND… *with This Answer…*

There are four reasons this night is different from all other nights. As you ask! We will answer! On this night we eat Matzah and Bitter Herbs, we dip, and we lean. When you learn what these strange things teach us, you will know why tonight is different from all other nights.

מה נשתנה

The Children Ask 'Mah Nishtanah'
Mah nishtanah ha lailah hazeh mikol ha leilot?

> « Call the children forward now. It is time to line up to ask the four questions from youngest to oldest. Answering the four questions is both a sacred act and a privilege.

THE FIRST CHILD ASKS...
What makes this night different from all other nights? On all other nights we do not dip even once, and on this night, we dip twice!

Sheb'khol haleilot ein anu matbilin afilu pa'am ehat; halailah hazeh, shtei f'amim.

THE SECOND CHILD ASKS...
On all other nights we eat leavened bread or matzah, and on this night, we eat only matzah!

Sheb'khol haleilot anu okhlin hametz umatzah; halailah hazeh, kuloh matzah.

THE THIRD CHILD ASKS...
On all other nights we eat all kinds of vegetables, and on this night, bitter herbs!

Sheb'khol haleilot anu okhlin sh'ar y'rakot; halailah hazeh, maror.

THE FOURTH CHILD ASKS...
On all other nights we eat sitting upright or reclining, and on this night we all lean back and recline!

Sheb'khol haleilot anu okhlin bein yoshvin uvein m'subin; halailah hazeh, kulanu m'subin.

The Four Questions In Hebrew

מַה נִּשְׁתַּנָּה הַלַּיְלָה הַזֶּה מִכָּל הַלֵּילוֹת? שֶׁבְּכָל הַלֵּילוֹת אָנוּ אוֹכְלִין חָמֵץ וּמַצָּה, הַלַּיְלָה הַזֶּה – כֻּלּוֹ מַצָּה. שֶׁבְּכָל הַלֵּילוֹת אָנוּ אוֹכְלִין שְׁאָר יְרָקוֹת – הַלַּיְלָה הַזֶּה (כֻּלּוֹ) מָרוֹר. שֶׁבְּכָל הַלֵּילוֹת אֵין אָנוּ מַטְבִּילִין אֲפִילוּ פַּעַם אֶחָת – הַלַּיְלָה הַזֶּה שְׁתֵּי פְעָמִים. שֶׁבְּכָל הַלֵּילוֹת אָנוּ אוֹכְלִין בֵּין יוֹשְׁבִין וּבֵין מְסֻבִּין – הַלַּיְלָה הַזֶּה כֻּלָּנוּ מְסֻבִּין.

Did you know?
- ζ It is both a sacred act and a privilege to answer the four questions of Passover. We answer and recall to the children the mighty works of the Almighty God. He is the one who keeps His Promises. Mah Nishtanah, the four questions, is a gift to every parent, an opening door to share their own connection to God with their children. And for every child, it gives them a special time to ask, ask, ask, ask.

- ζ What unique power does this night hold to inspire the souls of the living from generation to generation. God calls us all to his table tonight, He feeds us all. We should all come hungry to feel God near to us. Tonight, is for all those who ask why.

- ζ The Mah Nishtanah asks one question four ways. Why is tonight different from all other nights? The four questions are designed to give one answer to every person who seeks an answer.

- ζ We all ask why am I here, why me, why God. Each of us discovers the wonders of God in our own way. One curious discovery about God is that He truly loves us. It is He who created each of us intentionally different by design, making uniformity between us impossible. Yet, His word encourages us to be intentionally unified. It seems evident we were created to learn how to love. It is His plan to diligently be our God, to teach us of His love, and to deliver us from our bondage through His acts of love. We see this in His love for a people He made His own. Then, through them He sent His love to the whole world.

מַצָּה
THE MATZAH
Unleavened Bread

'And you shall observe this as an eternal ordinance
To you and your sons forever.'
EXODUS 12:24

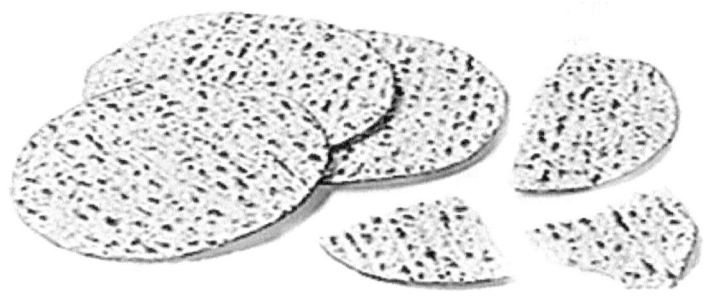

LEADER
On all other nights we eat bread with leaven, but on Passover we eat only unleavened Matzah. As the Israelites fled Egypt, they did not have time for their dough to rise. As they prepared to flee, they left their bread lay flat to bake in the hot desert sun.

ALL RESPOND
'Don't you know that a little leaven will work through the whole batch of dough? Get rid of the old leaven so that you may become who you really are now, a new batch with no leaven. For Messiah, Our Passover Lamb, has been sacrificed.' I Corinthians 5:7

« Lifting the plate with the three Matzah to say

LEADER

This is the bread of affliction, the poor bread which Israel ate in the land of Egypt. Let all who are hungry come and eat. Let all who are in need come and share in the hope of Passover.

LEADER
We can inspect the Matzah, we can see how it is striped.

ALL RESPOND
'He was wounded for our transgressions, and bruised for our iniquities, the chastisement of our peace was upon him, and by his stripes we are healed.' Isaiah 53:5

LEADER
We can touch the Matzah, we can feel how it is pierced.

ALL RESPOND
'And I will pour out upon the house of David, and upon the inhabitants of Jerusalem, the spirit of grace and of supplications, and they shall look upon me whom they have pierced, and they shall mourn for him as one mourns for an only son. And grieve as one grieves for His firstborn.' Zechariah 12:10

LEADER
As part of the Passover Seder, three pieces of Matzah are wrapped together in a cloth. Each piece in a separate section, yet joined as one. Some Rabbi's call these three 'a unity'.

They consider them to represent a unity of the three patriarchs, Abraham, Isaac, and Jacob. Messianic Believers consider this unity of three to be the image of the Father, the Son, and the Holy Spirit, joined as one.

During this season of Passover, let us break our old habits of sin and selfishness. Breaking free from our bondages and beginning a fresh, new and holy life.

Did you know?...

- If we examine the matzah, it is easy to see it is unleavened, pierced and striped.

- In Psalm 22, King David writes the following prophetic words in verses 15 through 19.

  My speech and my tongue cleave to the roof of my mouth. You have laid me to root in the dust of hades with the dead. The yelping dogs surround me to attack.

  A wicked mob gathers around me, they have pierced my hands and my feet. I can count all my bones. People stare as they gloat over me.

  They divide my clothes among themselves. They throw dice for my clothing as they divide my garments between themselves.

  O LORD, my strength, do not be so far away. Come quickly to help me LORD.

- How was it possible for Israel's King David to know this would become the testimony of Yeshua more than 1,000 years before it actually ever happened?

יחץ
YACHATZ
Breaking The Middle Matzah

Yeshua took the Matzah, blessed it and broke it, saying take and eat, this is my body which is given for you.

Do this to remember me.

MARK 14:22 ~ LUKE 22:19

LEADER

Now we will separate the middle matzah on the plate of three pieces, and brake it in half. The Left half is put back with the three. While the Right half is wrapped in a white linen cloth and designated as the Afikoman. This Right half, the Afikoman, will be set aside or hidden; only to be found at the end of the meal. The Afikoman is considered a dessert or reward at the end of the Passover.

It is a tradition to hide the Afikoman from the children, then send them off to find it later. With all the children's eyes covered, the Afikoman is hidden. Later, when the children find the Afikoman, it is returned to the Father. The child who finds it asks the Father to pay a ransom for the Afikoman, thus assuring its safe return. Then our Passover Seder is complete.

Matzah is called the Bread of Affliction. As it is broken and divided here, Yeshua was broken for us. He restored our division from the Father, making us a free people.

As this Matzah is divided from the other three, it becomes the Afikoman, meaning 'The Coming One.'

Finally, the divided half of Matzah has been wrapped in a white cloth and hidden. Yeshua's body was also wrapped in burial cloths, and hidden in a tomb.

Leader

Then as Yeshua was set apart in a burial cave at the beginning of the Passover, so too is our Afikoman wrapped and set apart. Both have been broken, divided, striped, pierced, wrapped, set apart, searched for, found, redeemed, and restored to The Father.

All of this reminds us of the sinless Messiah who rose from the dead, ascended into heaven, and restored the division between God and Sinners. Our every debt paid in full. When the division was restored in heaven, so it was on earth, and all are invited to partake.

- « Remove the half of Matzah remaining with the three pieces.

- « Divide the remaining Left half, breaking it up and sharing it with all the guests.

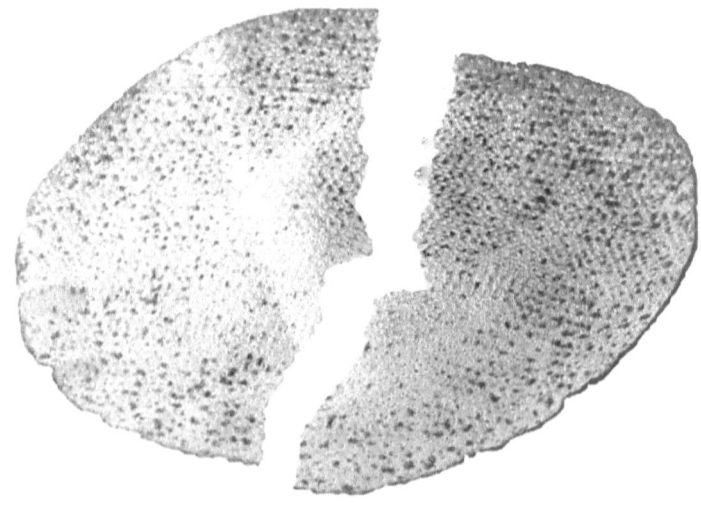

LEADER
Let us share in this unleavened bread of The Passover.

ALL RESPOND
Blessed are you, O Lord our God, Ruler of the Universe, who brings forth bread from the earth.

Baruch Atah, Adonai Elo-heinu, Melech Ha-olam, hamotzi leekhem min ha'aretz

בָּרוּךְ אַתָּה ה', אֱ-לֹהֵינוּ מֶלֶךְ הָעוֹלָם, הַמּוֹצִיא לֶחֶם מִן הָאָרֶץ.

Did you know?

ζ Jesus said, 'Truly I tell you that Moses did not give you the bread from heaven to eat. But it is my Father who gives you the true bread from heaven. God's bread is the man who comes from heaven and gives life to the world.'

ζ His disciples answered, 'Give us this bread forever.'

ζ Jesus then told them, 'I am the bread of life. Whoever comes to me will never hunger.' Then he said, 'Whoever believes will never be thirsty again. I am the living bread that came down from heaven, if any one eats of this bread, they shall live forever, and not die. The bread I will give is my body, which I will give for the life of the world.'

ζ

MAROR

The Bitter Herbs

And their lives were embittered with hard bondage.
EXODUS 1:14

LEADER

On all other nights we eat all kinds of vegetables, but tonight we eat bitter herbs to remember how bitter life was for the Israelites in Egypt. On all other nights we eat all kinds of vegetables. But on Passover we eat only Maror.

In the Mishnah, Pesachim 116b, it gives the reason for eating Maror. We eat Maror because the Egyptians embittered the lives of our forefathers while they were slaves in Egypt.

Pharaoh put slave drivers over the Israelites, who made them build the great cities for Pharaoh. They ruthlessly forced them into harder labor. They drove them bitterly into every kind of brutally hard work.

Let us scoop some Maror onto a piece of Matzah and allow its bitter taste to bring us to shed tears of compassion for the sorrow that our ancestors experienced while in bondage for over 400 years.

All Respond
Blessed are You, O Lord our God, Ruler of the Universe, who has set us apart by His Word and commanded us to eat bitter herbs.

Baruch Atah, Adonai Elo-heinu, Melech Ha-olam, asher kidshanu bidevaro vetzivanu al akhilar maror

» *NOW ALL EAT*, the Maror, the Bitter Herbs and Matzah

Did you Know?

- ζ Do you wonder why we are eating this stuff? Well, You're on to something there. During the Passover Seder, we ask that very question. The text of the Haggadah answers us by quoting a verse from the Torah, 'They embittered our lives with hard work.' The bitter taste of the herbs reminds us of the bitterness of our slavery in Egypt.

- ζ The actual source of the biblical commandment to eat Maror is found in a later verse, where God commands us to prepare the paschal lamb, then he says, 'Eat the lamb with the Matzah and Maror.'

- ζ The phraseology of this command is very precise: eating the Maror is a part of the mitzvah of eating the paschal lamb. Rather than being an independent mitzvah, it is actually a prerequisite for partaking of the paschal lamb.

- ζ Accordingly, since we no longer have the obligation to offer the paschal lamb because there is no Temple. There is no biblical command to eat Maror. However, even though the biblical notion of eating Maror to remember our slavery no longer applies, the Rabbis decreed that we should continue to eat Maror to remember and teach our children, what happened in Egypt, and how we remembered it in the days of The Temple.

חֲרוֹסֶת
KORECH & CHAROSET
We Dip Twice

Taste and see that The LORD is good.
Blessed is the person who takes refuge in him.
PSALM 34:8

LEADER
The Korech, a sandwich with Charoset, reminds us of the clay mixture used to make the bricks of Egypt. The Israelites toiled to make Egypt's treasured cities when Pharaoh demanded they make the clay bricks without straw. The Israelites grieved in their labor as they spent their lives building for gods who provided them nothing. We too have spent our lives working hard, only to build our lives out of strange clay.

ALL RESPOND
Let us taste and see that The Lord is good. He is sweet to the taste. He cares for us as the apple of his eye. He gives us what we need to rebuild our lives firmly. It is his kindness over us that leads us back to him.

LEADER
Let us all dip twice. With a piece of Maror, bitter herb, dip once again in the tears, then once in Charoset, the sweet apple clay. Let us scoop some Charoset onto our Matzah and pair it with the twice dipped Maror, making a Korech, because life with God turns the bitter to sweet.

« *NOW ALL EAT*, The Charoset with the twice dipped Maror

Why Do We All Recline Tonight?

Then as Yeshua instructed, the disciples went to the city, and they prepared the Passover. When it was evening, Yeshua and the Twelve were reclining and eating.
MARK 14:16-18

LEADER

It is a Passover mitzvah to remember and embrace these events and miracles of our Exodus from Egypt. We teach through our actions, we recline to show we have been emancipated. In this we act with tangible respect for the hospitality of God as we recline at His table. This we do to teach our children to live the life they see us living.

Reclining is symbolic of being a free people, on Pesach we remember our freedom by eating while at rest reclining. This Romanesque custom is mentioned as an instruction to remember in the Mishnah, at no other time are we mandated to recline as we eat. All other nights we eat as we will, but tonight we eat reclined and free.

The children of Israel were instructed to eat the Passover in haste, their loins girded, their staffs in hand, sandals upon their feet as they awaited departure from Egypt and its bondage. Today we are free, tonight we recline and freely enjoy the Passover Seder.

ALL RESPOND

Once we were slaves, but now we are free! Messiah said, 'Come unto me, all you who are weary and burdened, and I will give you rest. Take my yoke upon your shoulders and learn from me, I am gentle and humble. Find your rest in me. My yoke is easy and my burden is light.'

גִּיד

MAGGID
The Story of Passover

Salvation, power, the kingdom of our God and the authority
of his Messiah have come. The Accuser who torments them
day and night has been thrown down.
They overcame him by the Blood of The Lamb
and the Word of His Testimony.
REVELATION 12:10-11

READER ~ PORTION ONE

The Torah says we are to speak these words before God and say, 'My father was a wandering Aramean. When He went to Egypt, there were only a few of them. These few became a large and powerful nation. The Egyptians treated us harshly, making us do back breaking work for them. We cried out in our oppression and God heard us. He saw our misery and our suffering.

With his powerful arm and his mighty hand, he took us out of Egypt. He fought for us with wonderous signs and awesome deeds to set us free. He brought us to this place, and gave us our own land that was rich and overflowing with milk and honey. Our father in faith, Abraham, and his wife Sarah, left their home to travel to Canaan, where he became the father of a Great Nation. God told Abraham, 'Your descendants will be strangers in a strange land. They will be enslaved and oppressed for four hundred years. But I tell you, in the end, I will judge their oppressors.'

READER ~ PORTION TWO
Abraham's grandson, Jacob and his family, went down to Egypt at a time of famine in the land. Yet, while in Egypt, Jacob and the Israelites lived prosperously till a new Pharaoh rose up and said, 'There are too many Israelites, they are too mighty for us. Let us treat them harshly to weaken them before they grow stronger than us. What if war breaks out and they join our enemies to fight against us. Let's do what we must to stop them!

The Egyptian taskmasters forced them into hard labor, making them build cities for Pharaoh. Egypt embittered the Israelites lives with oppressive work. But still they continued to increase in numbers and in power. Over time, the Egyptians grew to despise them. Finally, Pharaoh ordered every Hebrew boy to be taken from his family, and thrown into the Nile River to drown.

READER ~ PORTION THREE
God remembered the covenant that he made with Abraham and Sarah. He called to Moses, telling him to appear before Pharaoh and demand that the Hebrew people be released from bondage. But Pharaoh refused to free Israel. Nine times Moses and his brother Aaron stood before Pharaoh and asked, 'Let My People Go', and each time Pharaoh refused. Each time God too answered Pharaoh, by sending a plague to the gods of Egypt.

After the ninth plague, God told Moses, 'Gather the elders of Israel, tell them to mark the tops and side posts of their doors with the blood of a lamb. This mark will seal your doors, and I will not let the destroyer come into your homes. And, do not let your families go out of your houses until the light of morning. Tonight, God will pass through all the land to smite every firstborn of Egypt.' The Lord has said, 'I will bring judgement on all the gods of Egypt, I am The Lord.' The blood of the lamb will be a sign to The Lord to pass over your doors.

Reader ~ Portion Four

It is written that God allowed the hardening of Pharaoh's heart each time Moses was sent to plead with him. Only after God sent Moses to plead with Pharaoh nine times did God release the tenth plague upon Egypt.

On that night, a great cry went up from all the land as the final plague, filled with death, entered the land. The Lord himself came to judge Egypt, taking away the breath of life from every firstborn throughout the land.

Only after death struck in the palace of Pharaoh did he surrender to God. Then Pharaoh called for Moses, and said, Take God's people out of Egypt, deliver them to a land God gives them, I will let God's people go!

All Respond

Then The Lord said to Moses, 'Tell this to the people, after you have entered the land that I have promised you. You and your children must continue to observe The Passover every year, forever.'

And when your children ask, 'What is this feast we are celebrating tonight?' You will teach them, 'Tonight, we remember the sacrifice of The Lord's Lamb. We do this to honor The Lord, who passed over our homes in Egypt, and did not smite us along with the firstborns of the Egyptians.

God divided us as a people and made us his own. He delivered us from the curse of death, he saved our children from the destroyer, and he set us all free.'

And after the Israelites heard these words from God, the children of God bowed their heads low, kneeled down and worshipped The Lord.

Only One God
Is Faithful & Able To Keep His Promises

Did you know?...

ζ Here we see Men of Israel gather around this Crowned Torah for the Priestly Blessing during the Passover at the Western Wall in Jerusalem.

ζ For more than 3200 years, Israel, the Children of God still keep The Passover throughout the world. They teach The Story to their children, they answer the four questions, and now they worship in their Promised Land again.

ζ So tell them, 'This is what The Almighty Lord says, I will bring Israel back together from the nations, and gather them from the countries where I have scattered them. I will give them the land of Israel.' This was the prophecy of Ezekiel in 11:17.

ζ I will gather those who remain, who are My flock, out of all the countries where I have driven them, and I will bring them back to the fold, and they will be fruitful and multiply. This was the prophecy of Jeremiah in 23:3.

ζ He will raise a sign like a flag for the nations to gather around. He will gather the outcasts of Israel and bring together the scattered people of Judah from the four corners of the earth. This was the prophecy of Isaiah in 11:12.

CUP OF PLAGUES
IAM Judges The gods Of Egypt

God said to them, 'I am The LORD your God who brought you out of Egypt, and bondage. You will have no other gods than me. You will not make any carving, or images, of any other thing either in heaven or earth. You will not bow down or serve the things you or any man will make.
I AM, The Lord your God, I am a jealous God.'
EXODUS 20:1-5

LEADER

Moses left the wilderness to return to Pharaoh's palace, the vary place where he had been raised. He returned with the message that The Lord had given him. Tell Pharaoh, Let God's people go. God also warned Moses of the hard resistance he would encounter.

ALL RESPOND

Then God said, 'the king of Egypt will not let you go unless a mighty hand forces him. I will stretch out my hand against Egypt with powerful wonders, that I will do among them. Afterward, Pharaoh will let you go.'

LEADER

'On that same night I will pass through Egypt, striking down every firstborn, both men and creature, I will execute judgment on the gods of Egypt. I am The Lord.'

A full Cup is a symbol of joy. Let us fill our cups again, but not drink yet. On Passover, we are filled with the joy of God's deliverance as we are saddened by the cost of our deliverance. Lives were lost, plagues poured out, sacrifices, blood, and even death. We also remember the price paid for the salvation of the world. The Lord gave to us, Messiah Yeshua, who was and is The Lamb of God. God too paid a precious price.

LEADER

Before we drink our cup filled with joy, we recount the Ten Plagues, the cost of idolatry. We dip our little finger into our cup, and remove a drop for each plague. Then we allow each drop to fall away. We see and remember how idolatry reduces the fullness of our Joy.

« Let each drop fall to your plate as you name each plague aloud.

ALL RESPOND ALOUD

BLOOD   FROGS
LICE   FLIES
DEAD LIVESTOCK
BOILS   HAIL
LOCUST   DARKNESS
DEATH OF THE FIRSTBORNS

The gods Of The Ten Plagues

≈ 1 ~ **Khnum**, the water god. God turned the Nile River into blood, including all its tributaries and other waters. All marine life died, and the stench of death filled Egypt. Egypt was without drinkable or any other potable water. Exodus 17:14-25

≈ 2 ~ **Heqet**, the fertility goddess. God provoked the frogs to come out of the waters and invade the dry land, they were in their homes and courtyards, and in the fields. There, the frogs died and rotted, till the whole land stank of them. Exodus 8:1-5

≈ 3 ~ **Seb**, the earth god. God called forth the dust of the earth to be change into gnats and lice. They infested all flesh with bites, tormenting the people and creatures throughout all of Egypt. Exodus 8:16-19

≈ 4 ~ **Khepri**, the god of flies. God sent swarms of flies to blanket the land. But not in the land of Goshen. God protected his people there, saying, 'I will separate your people from mine, so you will know, I, The Lord, am here in this land. Exodus 8:20-32

≈ 5 ~ **Hathor**, goddess of livestock. God struck Egypt's livestock with sickness and ultimately death. But He sent word to Pharaoh, 'I will spare the livestock of my people alone.' And so, He did. Exodus 9:1-7

≈ 6 ~ **Isis**, the goddess of wellbeing. God sent Moses and Aaron to show Pharaoh what God would do. Moses took a handful of the kilns ashes and threw it into the air, the ashes came down as a fine dust, causing skin boils and sores on all the people and creatures of Egypt. Exodus 9:8-12

≈ 7 ~ **Nut**, the goddess of sky. From the sky God sent thunder, hail, and lightning to strike the earth so harshly, that every person, animal, and plant left outside and uncovered was destroyed. Again, God protected his people in Goshen. Exodus 9:13-35

≈ 8 ~ **Seth**, the god of chaos. God sent a wind from the east to blow over Egypt all day and all night, and by morning the winds had delivered the locust to Egypt. The great swarm of locust ate all that was green, until nothing green was left on any tree or plant anywhere in Egypt. Exodus 10:13-15

≈ 9 ~ **Ra**, the god of the sun. God told Moses to lift his hand to the sky. Suddenly a complete darkness so thick it could be felt, fell over the land. Egypt lived in complete darkness for three days. But not so in Goshen, God gave them light.   Exodus 10:21-29

≈ 10 ~ **Pharaoh**, the god over all people. He believed he was destined to become the god of gods. But I AM, God himself, came to judge the gods of Egypt, and that included Pharaoh. Exodus 12:12

READER ~ PORTION ONE

The Lord kept his promise, every door covered with blood was the sign to The Lord, that house was protected from judgement. Those He found unmarked when He came, He allowed the destroyer to enter there, executing His judgement.

Beginning at midnight, death came for every firstborn male and creature throughout Egypt. Howling cries arose from every home; even from the courts of Pharaoh's Palace. Exodus 11:1-10, Exodus 12:29-32

The time had come when the ten plagues had passed, leaving Egypt completely broken. Pharaoh, considered to have divine power, was powerless against Almighty God. His sorcerers were powerless, and every deity was rendered powerless by the plagues God designed to destroy them all.

Reader ~ Portion Two

Their cattle were destroyed, their agriculture and economy destroyed, even their labor force of slaves were gone. The powerful nation of Egypt was broken spiritually, religiously, morally, and economically. By the time the Israelites began to exit, nothing that Egypt looked to for power was left. All that remained for Pharaoh to lean on was his army.

So, he pursued the Israelites with furious anger. With the hardest of hearts, he charged on in pursuit, only to lose all he had left. With a vengeful pride driving himself and his army, he plunged them all into their final destruction, the Red Sea.

Reader ~ Portion Three

Then God spoke this promise to Moses and to the people. 'Fear nothing, be brave, I will save you this day. Be still, and see the salvation, the Yeshua, of The Lord that only He can show you now. This enemy who relentlessly hunts you today, you will never see them again. Move Forward,' says The Lord. Exodus 14:13-15

קרבן פסח
Passover Lamb
God's Sacrifice
The Cost of Redemption

The blood that marks your doors will be a sign of protection over you. When I see the blood, I will pass over you. Nothing will touch you, nothing will strike you when I strike Egypt.
EXODUS 12:13

LEADER
Paul the Apostle, Rabbi Saul, was a student of esteemed 1st century Tzadik and scholar, Rabban Gamaliel. He taught that the Maggid must include three main truths.

> *The MATZAH ~ Unleavened Bread*
> *The MAROR ~ Bitter Herbs*
> *The BLOOD ~ Passover Lamb*

ZEROAH
The Shank Bone of a Lamb

LEADER
We have eaten the Matzah to remind us of the haste with which the children of Israel fled Egypt. We have tasted the Maror to remind us of the bitter slavery of Egypt. Now we remember the Passover Lamb through the Zeroah.

The Zeroah is the roasted shank bone of a lamb, it is a symbol of the Paschal Lamb. Reminding us of the sacrifice, and the blood that marks us as protected from the destroyer, and our separation from the curse of death.

Reader ~ Portion One

And The Lord said, 'On the tenth day of this month each man is to take a lamb for his family, one for each household. The animals you choose must be male yearlings without defect. Take care of them until the fourteenth day of the month. Then all the people of Israel must slaughter them at twilight. Then you are to take the blood and put it on the door frames of the houses where you will partake and eat the lambs.'

Reader ~ Portion Two

That same night they are to eat the meat roasted over the fire, along with bitter herbs and unleavened bread. This is how you are to eat it, with your cloak tucked into your belt, your sandals on your feet, and your staff in your hand. Eat it in haste, it is The Lord's Passover.

The blood will be a sign of protection on your houses, and when I see the blood, I will pass over you. I will not allow the destroyer to enter there when I strike Egypt.

Leader

We are reminded by Moses that it was The Lord Himself who redeemed the children of Israel from slavery. Moses said, 'The Lord brought us out of Egypt with a mighty hand and with His outstretched arm, with great terror with wonders and miraculous signs.'

It was The Lord who delivered us all… Let us read together and remember what The Lord has done for us.

Leader

On that same night I will pass through Egypt

All Respond

I, and not an angel

LEADER
And strike down every firstborn, both man and animals

ALL RESPOND
I, and not a seraph

LEADER
I will bring judgment on all the gods of Egypt

ALL RESPOND
I, and not a messenger

LEADER
Because, I am The Lord

ALL RESPOND
I myself and none other

BEITZAH
Roasted Egg as The Khagigah Offering

LEADER
The Zeroah reminds us of the Sacrificial Lamb of God, the Messiah. Even though a lamb is no longer roasted at Passover since the destruction of the Temple in Jerusalem. We now make a substitute offering with the Beitzah, a roasted egg, or Khagigah Offering.

> « Lift the Roasted Egg from the Seder Plate as you explain about the role of the egg. *The roasted egg is eaten later during the Passover Supper.*

LEADER
This roasted egg is now added to the Seder Plate, we call it Khagigah, which means 'The Special Holiday Offering'.

LEADER

The Beitzah, roasted egg, is a symbol of mourning that reminds us of the destruction of the Temple. It also reminds us of the new birth; its shape with no beginning and no end reminds us of eternal life.

ALL RESPOND

We who have trusted in Yeshua the Messiah, believe he is the Lamb of God, who he himself was sent for us.

Like the ancient Israelites,
We know that it was God Himself, and not an angel.
It was God Himself and not a seraph.
It was God Himself, and not a messenger,
Who won our final redemption from sin and death.

It is God Himself, through Yeshua,
Who takes away the sins of the world.

Did you know?...
- Isaiah prophesied about a Suffering Servant of Israel to come, saying, 'He grew up in His presence like a young tree, like a root out of dry ground. He had no form or majesty that would make us look at him. He had nothing in his appearance that would make us want him. He was despised and rejected by all people. He was a man familiar with sorrows, familiar with suffering. He was despised like those whom people turn their faces away from, we didn't consider him to be worth of anything.

    It is He who certainly has carried and taken upon himself our suffering and our sorrows, and for that we thought that God had wounded him, beat him, and punished him. He was wounded for our rebellious acts. He was crushed for our sins. He was punished so that we could have peace, and we received healing from his wounds. We have all strayed away like sheep. Each one of us has turned to live our own way, and for that, The LORD has laid all of our sins on him. Isaiah 53:2-6

DAYENU
It Would Have Been Enough

God is with you, He is the Hero who saves you.
Happily, He rejoices over you, renewing you with His love,
celebrating over you with His songs of joy.
ZEPHANIAH 3:17

LEADER

We conclude telling the story of Passover with a song. A poetic recounting of all the wonderful works God performed for the Israelites in Egypt.

The song is known as Dayenu, meaning, 'It Would Have Been Enough.' Each time we sing the word, Dayenu, we remember the abundant mercy He pours over Israel, as He pours over us today.

If The Lord had done only one of His wonderful works, and nothing more, it would have been enough to deliver and bless us, and more than enough to save us forever.

Dayenu

Phonetic Hebrew Version

The Verse

> *Ilu ho-tsi, Ho-tsi-a-nu,*
> *Ho-tsi-anu, Mi-Mitz-ra-yim*
> *Ho-tsi-anu, Mi-Mitz-ra-yim*
> *Da-ye-nu*

The Chorus

> *Da-da-ye-nu, Da-da-ye-nu,*
> *Da-da-ye-nu, Da-da-ye-nu,*
> *Da-ye-un, Da-ye-nu*

Dayenu ~ *English Version Read Aloud as Poetic Verse*

If God would've taken us out of Egypt,
and not executed judgment upon them,
It would've been enough, *Dayenu*.

If He would've executed judgment upon them,
and not upon their idols,
It would've been enough, *Dayenu*.

If He would've judged their idols,
and not killed their firstborn,
It would've been enough, *Dayenu*.

If He would've killed their firstborn,
and not given us their wealth,
It would've been enough, *Dayenu*.

If He would've given us their wealth,
and not split the sea for us,
It would've been enough, *Dayenu*.

If He would've split the sea for us,
and not led us through the sea on dry land,
It would've been enough, *Dayenu*.

If He would've led us through the sea on dry land,
and not drowned our enemies in the sea,
It would've been enough, *Dayenu*.

If He would've drowned our enemies in the sea,
and not provided for our needs in the desert for 40 years,
It would've been enough, *Dayenu*.

How great is God's goodness to us.
For each of His acts of mercy and kindness,
We declare *Dayenu — it would have been enough!*

SHULKHAN OREYKH
The Passover Supper
And you will keep it as a feast to The Lord forever.
EXODUS 12:14

LEADER ~ *A Prayer over the Passover Meal.*

Blessed are You, Lord our God, King of the Universe,
who brings forth bread from the earth.

Baruch Atah, Adonai Elo-heinu, Melech Ha-olam,
hamotzi lechem min ha-aretz.

With Praise and Thanksgiving

ALL RESPOND
We thank The Holy One, blessed be He,
He provided all these blessings for our ancestors.
And not only these, but so many more.
Blessed are You, O Lord our God,

For You have, in your mercy, supplied all our needs.
You have given us Messiah, and forgiveness of sins,
Life abundant and life everlasting. Hallelujah!

AFIKOMAN
God's Hidden Treasure

And when you seek me, you will find me,
when you search for me with all your heart.
JEREMIAH 29:13

LEADER

It is time to search for the Afikoman. It is a highlight of the evening when the Afikoman is found and ransomed by the head of the table. Whoever finds it presents it to the Leader. It is 'The Redeemer' who rejoins it to its broken half before offering all a piece of the Afikoman.

This is the final food of the Passover. We share it as a family, just as the Passover Lamb was shared before the Exodus. As Yeshua shared it with his Disciples.

» Encourage the children to search with care and joy! Make it joyful and fun as you help them ask, knock, seek, and find.

The Afikoman should linger in our mouth, meaningful and sweet to the taste. It was the Afikomen that Yeshua pointed to and said, 'This is my body given for you. When you do this remember me.' Now, let us share this Afikoman and remember the broken body of the Lamb of God who takes away our sins and the sins of the world.

ALL RESPOND

Blessed are You, O Lord our God, King of the Universe, who brings forth bread from the earth.

Baruch Atah, Adonai Elo-heinu, Melech Ha-olam, hamotzi lekhem min ha'aretz

קַדֵּשׁ
KADESH
CUP OF REDEMPTION
For The New Covenant

I will redeem you with my outstretched arm
and with great judgements.
EXODUS 6:6

LEADER
Let us fill our cups for the third time. This is the Cup of Redemption. It is symbolic of the blood of The Passover Lamb. It was with this cup Yeshua identified himself as Messiah.

ALL RESPOND
I will redeem you with my outstretched arm.

LEADER
'Surely the arm of The Lord is not too short to save,' said Isaiah. 'It is our sin that separates us from The Lord. We caused The Lord to search for one to help us, but He found no one worthy to help us. So, The Lord Himself helped us.

It was The Lords arm that stretch out to save us. It is The Lord alone who holds us tightly, victoriously, and wholly.

Yeshua took this same cup and said, 'This is the cup of the New Covenant made with my blood, which is poured out for you.' Just as the blood of the lamb brought salvation to Israel in Egypt, so Messiah's death makes atonement for all who believe, and offers salvation to whosoever will believe him.

ALL RESPOND
Blessed are you, O Lord our God, Ruler of the Universe, who creates the fruit of the vine.

Baruch Atah, Adonai Elo-heinu, Melech Ha-olam, boreh pree ha-ga-fen

בָּרוּךְ אַתָּה ה', אֱ-לֹהֵינוּ מֶלֶךְ הָעוֹלָם, בּוֹרֵא פְּרִי הַגָּפֶן.

Did you know?...
- The first is the Cup of Sanctification
  To Remember He has set us all apart

  The second is the Cup of Wrath
  To Remember He sent the plagues upon their gods

  The third is the Cup of Redemption
  To Remember He made them a Holy Nation

  The fourth is the Cup of Praise
  To Remember He alone is Worthy
  He alone is God

קָדֵשׁ
KADESH
CUP OF ELIJAH
For The Prophet Eliyahu Ha Navi

Watch, I will send to you the Prophet Elijah
Before the coming dreadful Day of The LORD.
MALACHI 4:5

LEADER
The Final Act has come, it is time to address The Fifth Cup, filled and ready, set apart for the Prophet Elijah. It is Elijah who will come to announce the Day of The Messiah's arrival. He will come as one sent from God.

We lift the cup from Elijah's place at the table. Only Elijah, Eliyahu Ha Navi, will fulfil the prophecy of announcing to the world the coming of our Messiah.

ALL RESPOND
The Lord will send you the prophet Elijah before that great and dreadful day of The Lords coming.

LEADER
Elijah did not see death, he was swept up to heaven by a great whirlwind in a chariot of fire. It is our hope to see Elijah come tonight to announce the long-awaited arrival of The Messiah, Son of David.

Before the birth of John, the Baptizer, an angel of The Lord said, 'And he will go on before The Lord, in the spirit and power of Elijah, making the people ready and prepared for The Lord to come.'

LEADER

Yeshua said about John, 'if you are willing to believe it, he is the Elijah who was to come.' It was this John, who when he saw Yeshua, declared, 'Look, the Lamb of God who takes away the sins of the world.'

קַדֵּשׁ
KADESH
CUP OF PRAISE
The Great Hallel

I will take you as my own people,
And I will be your God.
EXODUS 6:7

LEADER
Let us lift our cups one last time. Giving thanks to God, our Great Redeemer. For His love endures forever.

ALL RESPOND
Blessed are you, O Lord our God, Ruler of the Universe, who creates the fruit of the vine. Let us gratefully drink.

Baruch Atah, Adonai Elo-heinu, Melech Ha-olam, boreh pree ha-ga-fen

בָּרוּךְ אַתָּה ה׳, אֱ-לֹהֵינוּ מֶלֶךְ הָעוֹלָם, בּוֹרֵא פְּרִי הַגָּפֶן.

~ ~ A Meditation of Praise ~ ~
Praise The Lord who is set apart, I will bless Him as long as I live.
Praise The Lord with lifted hands, Praise His holy name.
Praise The Lord for His commandments, and His word which I love.
Praise The Lord and meditate on His statutes.
Praise The Lord sitting high and lifted up,
Let the hem of His garment fill the temple.
Praise The Lord again, in every season, at all times.
The Lord alone is enthroned upon the Praises of His people.

Psalm 22:3 ~ Psalm 63:4 ~ Psalm 119:43 ~ Psalm 34:1 ~ Isaiah 6:1

Psalm 136 ~ The Great Hallel

Give thanks to the Lord, for he is good,
> *His love endures forever.*

Give thanks to the God of gods,
> *His love endures forever.*

Give thanks to the Lord of lords,
> *His love endures forever.*

To him who alone does great wonders,
> *His love endures forever.*

Who by his understanding made the heavens,
> *His love endures forever.*

Who spread out the earth upon the waters,
> *His love endures forever.*

Who made the great lights,
> *His love endures forever.*

The sun to govern the day,
> *His love endures forever.*

The moon and stars to govern the night,
> *His love endures forever.*

To him who struck down the firstborn of Egypt,
> *His love endures forever.*

And brought Israel out from among them,
> *His love endures forever.*

With a mighty hand and outstretched arm,
> *His love endures forever.*

To him who divided the Red Sea asunder,
> *His love endures forever.*

And brought Israel through the midst of it,
> *His love endures forever.*

But swept Pharaoh and his army into the Red Sea,
> *His love endures forever.*

NIRTZAH
It Is Finished

Let all things be done decently and in order.
1 CORINTHIANS 14:40

LEADER
Our journey is complete, just as our own redemption is forever complete. We have finished the Passover Seder according to its precepts and customs. We have come to the conclusion of the official order of the Seder.

Let us pray for peace as we conclude our evening with the traditional confession of hope that we may celebrate The Passover next year in Jerusalem.

ALL RESPOND
O Lord, bring Messiah to the world through us now.
Order our steps as if they were His.
May we live in the Shalom of Your Presence.
And we ask you that you cover Jerusalem in Your Peace.

Lishana Ba'Haah Bi Yerushalim

Next Year in Jerusalem!

Lishana Ba'Haah Bi Yerushalim

Until next year, May we all dwell in peace! Jeremiah 24:4-7

The Aaronic Blessing ~ The Birkat Kohanim
The Lord Bless you and Keep You
The Lord make his face to shine upon you
And be gracious to you
The Lord lift up his countenance upon you
And give you peace

ζ The Aaronic Blessing, or Priestly Blessing ~ The Birkat Kohanim
   was given as God's Blessing over His people in Numbers 6:24-26

Additional Ministry Resources available by contacting
Metro Jewish Resources.
P.O. Box 3777 ~ Wayne, NJ 07474

MJR on the internet
www.metrojesishag.org

MJR via email
metrojrag@gmail.com

MJR phone HQ Missions Office
1-973-461-9786

Additional Passover Haggadah's
Available through the MJR Missions Office

For Passover Seder planning Q&A and assistance on
How to Host a large gathering or outreach,
contact the Metro Jewish Resources
mission's office by email or phone asap.

Other resources available through MJR
Articles & Books
Training Materials
Ambassador Program
Jewish Testimonies
MJR Outreaches

www.ingramcontent.com/pod-product-compliance
Lightning Source LLC
Chambersburg PA
CBHW022000290426
44108CB00012B/1144